Teacup and Saucer

Keith N. Ferreira

iUniverse, Inc.
Bloomington

Teacup and Saucer

iUniverse books may be ordered through booksellers or by contacting:

iUniverse
1663 Liberty Drive
Bloomington, IN 47403
www.iuniverse.com
1-800-Authors (1-800-288-4677)

ISBN: 978-1-4620-1305-0 (sc)
ISBN: 978-1-4620-1278-7 (ebk)

Printed in the United States of America

iUniverse rev. date: 05/03/2011

Books by Keith N. Ferreira

The Intellectual Rebel
Aphorisms
Speculative Aphorisms
Speculative Aphorisms II
Philoscience
Philoscience II
Intellectual Jazz
Intellectual Jazz II
Jazzism
Neoliberal Arts
Neoliberal Arts II
Postmodern Minimalist Philosophy
Simpletism
Uncertaintyism
The Ultimate Truth
Anything Is Possible
Political and Social Observations
The University of Neoliberal Arts
A New Breed of Philosophers
Ferreirism - The Ultimate Philosophy
The eChurch of Zerotropy
The Ferreira Genesis Equation
Zerotropism and Panaceanism

Philosophy Should Belong to the Masses
Programming the World with Philosophy
The Masses Should Think for Themselves
The Masses Educated Can Never Be Defeated
All of My Violet eGoddesses Are My Wives

Please visit my website at: ***http://www.philophysics.com***

Thank You!

Teacup and Saucer (Part One)

Teacup and Saucer = True Cunt University of Philosophy and the (Flying) Saucer = The University of Neoliberal Arts! Teacup and Saucer = True Cunt University of Philosophy and the (Flying) Saucer = The University of Neoliberal Arts! Teacup and Saucer = True Cunt University of Philosophy and the (Flying) Saucer = The University of Neoliberal Arts! Thus speaks, Dr. Keith N. Ferreira of the University of Neoliberal Arts. Believe it or not! May the Source be with you! QED! (3/1/11)

Teacup and Saucer = True Cunt University of Philosophy and the (Flying) Saucer = The University of Neoliberal Arts! Teacup and Saucer = True Cunt University of Philosophy and the (Flying) Saucer = The University of Neoliberal Arts! Teacup and Saucer = True Cunt University of Philosophy and the (Flying) Saucer = The University of Neoliberal Arts! Thus speaks, Dr. Keith N. Ferreira of the University of Neoliberal Arts. Believe it or not! May the Source be with you! QED! (3/1/11)

Who are the ones that are telling people how to live their lives, and what are their motives for telling people how to live their lives? Who are the ones that are telling people how to live their lives, and what are their motives for telling people how to live their lives? Who are the ones that are telling people how to live their lives, and what are their motives for telling people how to live their lives? Thus speaks, Dr. Keith N. Ferreira of the University of Neoliberal Arts. Believe it or not! May the Source be with you! QED! (3/1/11)

Who are the ones that are telling people how to live their lives, and what are their motives for telling people how to live their lives? Who are the ones that are telling people how to live their lives, and what are their motives for telling people how to live their lives? Who are the ones that are telling people how to live their lives, and what are their motives for telling people how to live their lives? Thus speaks, Dr. Keith N. Ferreira of the University of Neoliberal Arts. Believe it or not! May the Source be with you! QED! (3/1/11)

Is making something of myself more important than what I am doing? Is making something of myself more important than what I am doing? Is making something of myself more important than what I am doing? Thus speaks, Dr. Keith N. Ferreira of the University of Neoliberal Arts. Believe it or not! May the Source be with you! QED! (3/1/11)

Is making something of myself more important than what I am doing? Is making something of myself more important than what I am doing? Is making something of myself more important than what I am doing? Thus speaks, Dr. Keith N. Ferreira of the University of Neoliberal Arts. Believe it or not! May the Source be with you! QED! (3/1/11)

Who are the ones that are telling people how to live their lives, and what are their motives for telling people how to live their lives? Who are the ones that are telling people how to live their lives, and what are their motives for telling people how to live their lives? Who are the ones that are telling people how to live their lives, and what are their motives for telling people how to live their lives? Thus speaks, Dr. Keith N. Ferreira of the University of Neoliberal Arts. Believe it or not! May the Source be with you! QED! (3/1/11)

Who are the ones that are telling people how to live their lives, and what are their motives for telling people how to live their lives? Who are the ones that are telling people how to live their lives, and what are their motives for telling people how to live their lives? Who are the ones that are telling people how to live their lives, and what are their motives for telling people how to live their lives? Thus speaks, Dr. Keith N. Ferreira of the University of Neoliberal Arts. Believe it or not! May the Source be with you! QED! (3/1/11)

Cosmetics = Cosmatics, and vice versa! Cosmetics = Cosmatics, and vice versa! Cosmetics = Cosmatics, and vice versa! Thus speaks, Dr. Keith N. Ferreira of the University of Neoliberal Arts. Believe it or not! May the Source be with you! QED! (3/1/11)

Cosmetics = Cosmatics, and vice versa! Cosmetics = Cosmatics, and vice versa! Cosmetics = Cosmatics, and vice versa! Thus speaks, Dr. Keith N. Ferreira of the University of Neoliberal Arts. Believe it or not! May the Source be with you! QED! (3/1/11)

Sine = Male, and Cosine = Female! Sine = Male, and Cosine = Female! Sine = Male, and Cosine = Female! Thus speaks, Dr. Keith N. Ferreira of the University of Neoliberal Arts. Believe it or not! May the Source be with you! QED! (3/1/11)

Sine = Male, and Cosine = Female! Sine = Male, and Cosine = Female! Sine = Male, and Cosine = Female! Thus speaks, Dr. Keith N. Ferreira of the University of Neoliberal Arts. Believe it or not! May the Source be with you! QED! (3/1/11)

The key to entering the mind of women is the words cosmetics and cosmatics! The key to entering the mind of women is the words cosmetics and cosmatics! The key to entering the mind of women is the words cosmetics and cosmatics! Thus speaks, Dr. Keith N. Ferreira of the University of Neoliberal Arts. Believe it or not! May the Source be with you! QED! (3/1/11)

The key to entering the mind of women is the words cosmetics and cosmatics! The key to entering the mind of women is the words cosmetics and cosmatics! The key to entering the mind of women is the words cosmetics and cosmatics! Thus speaks, Dr. Keith N. Ferreira of the University of Neoliberal Arts. Believe it or not! May the Source be with you! QED! (3/1/11)

Cosmetics = Cosine mathematics, when e = a! And, Smetics = Sine mathematics, when e = a! Cosmetics = Cosine mathematics, when e = a! And, Smetics = Sine mathematics, when e = a! Cosmetics = Cosine mathematics, when e = a! And, Smetics = Sine mathematics, when e = a! Thus speaks, Dr. Keith N. Ferreira of the University of Neoliberal Arts. Believe it or not! May the Source be with you! QED! (3/1/11)

Cosmetics = Cosine mathematics, when e = a! And, Smetics = Sine mathematics, when e = a! Cosmetics = Cosine mathematics, when e = a! And, Smetics = Sine mathematics, when e = a! Cosmetics = Cosine mathematics, when e = a! And, Smetics = Sine mathematics, when e = a! Thus speaks, Dr. Keith N. Ferreira of the University of Neoliberal Arts. Believe it or not! May the Source be with you! QED! (3/1/11)

E = A, when Electronics = Piece of ass. In other words, E = Electronics, and A = Ass! E = A, when Electronics = Piece of ass. In other words, E = Electronics, and A = Ass! E = A, when Electronics = Piece of ass. In other words, E = Electronics, and A = Ass! E = A, when Electronics = Piece of ass. In other words, E = Electronics, and A = Ass! Thus speaks, Dr. Keith N. Ferreira of the University of Neoliberal Arts. Believe it or not! May the Source be with you! QED! (3/1/11)

E = A, when Electronics = Piece of ass. In other words, E = Electronics, and A = Ass! E = A, when Electronics = Piece of ass. In other words, E = Electronics, and A = Ass! E = A, when Electronics = Piece of ass. In other words, E = Electronics, and A = Ass! E = A, when Electronics = Piece of ass. In other words, E = Electronics, and A = Ass! Thus speaks, Dr. Keith N. Ferreira of the University of Neoliberal Arts. Believe it or not! May the Source be with you! QED! (3/1/11)

Harem = Here mathematics is done, when a = e! And, Herem = Here sex is done, when e = a! In other words, Ass = Electronics, and vice versa! Therefore, Language = Electronics = Mathematics = Sex! Thus speaks, Dr. Keith N. Ferreira of the University of Neoliberal Arts. Believe it or not! May the Source be with you! QED! (3/1/11)

Harem = Here mathematics is done, when a = e! And, Herem = Here sex is done, when e = a! In other words, Ass = Electronics, and vice versa! Therefore, Language = Electronics = Mathematics = Sex! Thus speaks, Dr. Keith N. Ferreira of the University of Neoliberal Arts. Believe it or not! May the Source be with you! QED! (3/1/11)

Tea = Tangent electronics is about ass (sex)! Tea = Tangent electronics is about ass (sex)! Tea = Tangent electronics is about ass (sex)! Thus speaks, Dr. Keith N. Ferreira of the University of Neoliberal Arts. Believe it or not! May the Source be with you! QED! (3/2/11)

Tea = Tangent electronics is about ass (sex)! Tea = Tangent electronics is about ass (sex)! Tea = Tangent electronics is about ass (sex)! Thus speaks, Dr. Keith N. Ferreira of the University of Neoliberal Arts. Believe it or not! May the Source be with you! QED! (3/2/11)

Time = Tangent is my electronics! Time = Tangent is my electronics! Time = Tangent is my electronics! Thus speaks, Dr. Keith N. Ferreira of the University of Neoliberal Arts. Believe it or not! May the Source be with you! QED! (3/2/11)

Time = Tangent is my electronics! Time = Tangent is my electronics! Time = Tangent is my electronics! Thus speaks, Dr. Keith N. Ferreira of the University of Neoliberal Arts. Believe it or not! May the Source be with you! QED! (3/2/11)

"Time waits for no one!" "Time waits for no one!" "Time waits for no one!" Thus speaks, Dr. Keith N. Ferreira of the University of Neoliberal Arts. Believe it or not! May the Source be with you! QED! (3/2/11)

"Time waits for no one!" "Time waits for no one!" "Time waits for no one!" Thus speaks, Dr. Keith N. Ferreira of the University of Neoliberal Arts. Believe it or not! May the Source be with you! QED! (3/2/11)

People of the world: The Ferreira Fundamental Trinity is about electronics! People of the world: The Ferreira Fundamental Trinity is about electronics! People of the world: The Ferreira Fundamental Trinity is about electronics! Thus speaks, Dr. Keith N. Ferreira of the University of Neoliberal Arts. Believe it or not! May the Source be with you! QED! (3/2/11)

People of the world: The Ferreira Fundamental Trinity is about electronics! People of the world: The Ferreira Fundamental Trinity is about electronics! People of the world: The Ferreira Fundamental Trinity is about electronics! Thus speaks, Dr. Keith N. Ferreira of the University of Neoliberal Arts. Believe it or not! May the Source be with you! QED! (3/2/11)

One does not have to know advanced anything to be the best at anything! One does not have to know advanced anything to be the best at anything! One does not have to know advanced anything to be the best at anything! Thus speaks, Dr. Keith N. Ferreira of the University of Neoliberal Arts. Believe it or not! May the Source be with you! QED! (3/2/11)

One does not have to know advanced anything to be the best at anything! One does not have to know advanced anything to be the best at anything! One does not have to know advanced anything to be the best at anything! Thus speaks, Dr. Keith N. Ferreira of the University of Neoliberal Arts. Believe it or not! May the Source be with you! QED! (3/2/11)

ChapStick is for Chaps! ChapStick is for Chaps! ChapStick is for Chaps! Thus speaks, Dr. Keith N. Ferreira of the University of Neoliberal Arts. Believe it or not! May the Source be with you! QED! (3/2/11)

ChapStick is for Chaps! ChapStick is for Chaps! ChapStick is for Chaps! Thus speaks, Dr. Keith N. Ferreira of the University of Neoliberal Arts. Believe it or not! May the Source be with you! QED! (3/2/11)

ChapStick = Lip Balm = For chapped lips! ChapStick = Lip Balm = For chapped lips! ChapStick = Lip Balm = For chapped lips! Thus speaks, Dr. Keith N. Ferreira of the University of Neoliberal Arts. Believe it or not! May the Source be with you! QED! (3/2/11)

ChapStick = Lip Balm = For chapped lips! ChapStick = Lip Balm = For chapped lips! ChapStick = Lip Balm = For chapped lips! Thus speaks, Dr. Keith N. Ferreira of the University of Neoliberal Arts. Believe it or not! May the Source be with you! QED! (3/2/11)

Tan = Take (piece) of ass now! Tan = Take (piece) of ass now! Tan = Take (piece) of ass now! Thus speaks, Dr. Keith N. Ferreira of the University of Neoliberal Arts. Believe it or not! May the Source be with you! QED! (3/1/11)

Tan = Take (piece) of ass now! Tan = Take (piece) of ass now! Tan = Take (piece) of ass now! Thus speaks, Dr. Keith N. Ferreira of the University of Neoliberal Arts. Believe it or not! May the Source be with you! QED! (3/1/11)

Cunt = See you in time (tangent)! Cunt = See you in time (tangent)! Cunt = See you in time (tangent)! Thus speaks, Dr. Keith N. Ferreira of the University of Neoliberal Arts. Believe it or not! May the Source be with you! QED! (3/1/11)

Cunt = See you in time (tangent)! Cunt = See you in time (tangent)! Cunt = See you in time (tangent)! Thus speaks, Dr. Keith N. Ferreira of the University of Neoliberal Arts. Believe it or not! May the Source be with you! QED! (3/1/11)

Tangent = Tan gentleman/women/etc.! Tangent = Tan gentleman/women/etc.! Tangent = Tan gentleman/women/etc.! Thus speaks, Dr. Keith N. Ferreira of the University of Neoliberal Arts. Believe it or not! May the Source be with you! QED! (3/1/11)

Tangent = Tan gentleman/women/etc.! Tangent = Tan gentleman/women/etc.! Tangent = Tan gentleman/women/etc.! Thus speaks, Dr. Keith N. Ferreira of the University of Neoliberal Arts. Believe it or not! May the Source be with you! QED! (3/1/11)

Time = Tangent in mathematical electronics! Time = Tangent in mathematical electronics! Time = Tangent in mathematical electronics! Thus speaks, Dr. Keith N. Ferreira of the University of Neoliberal Arts. Believe it or not! May the Source be with you! QED! (3/1/11)

Time = Tangent in mathematical electronics! Time = Tangent in mathematical electronics! Time = Tangent in mathematical electronics! Thus speaks, Dr. Keith N. Ferreira of the University of Neoliberal Arts. Believe it or not! May the Source be with you! QED! (3/1/11)

Sex = Solving electronics unknowns! Sex = Solving electronics unknowns! Sex = Solving electronics unknowns! Thus speaks, Dr. Keith N. Ferreira of the University of Neoliberal Arts. Believe it or not! May the Source be with you! QED! (3/1/11)

Sex = Solving electronics unknowns! Sex = Solving electronics unknowns! Sex = Solving electronics unknowns! Thus speaks, Dr. Keith N. Ferreira of the University of Neoliberal Arts. Believe it or not! May the Source be with you! QED! (3/1/11)

The Neolaw of Entropy: $S = (k \log n) / (c \log 1/n)$, where S equals Entropy, k and c are adjustable constants, and n equals pure number! The Neolaw of Entropy: $S = (k \log n) / (c \log 1/n)$, where S equals Entropy, k and c are adjustable constants, and n equals pure number! The Neolaw of Entropy: $S = (k \log n) / (c \log 1/n)$, where S equals Entropy, k and c are adjustable constants, and n equals pure number! Thus speaks, Captain Keith N. Ferreira of the Jolly Roger 7. Believe it or not! May the Source be with you! QED! (3/14/11)

The Neolaw of Entropy: $S = (k \log n) / (c \log 1/n)$, where S equals Entropy, k and c are adjustable constants, and n equals pure number! The Neolaw of Entropy: $S = (k \log n) / (c \log 1/n)$, where S equals Entropy, k and c are adjustable constants, and n equals pure number! The Neolaw of Entropy: $S = (k \log n) / (c \log 1/n)$, where S equals Entropy, k and c are adjustable constants, and n equals pure number! Thus speaks, Captain Keith N. Ferreira of the Jolly Roger 7. Believe it or not! May the Source be with you! QED! (3/14/11)

Teacup and Saucer (Part Two)

Never judge a book until one has decoded the book for oneself = Women! Never judge a book until one has decoded the book for oneself = Women! Never judge a book until one has decoded the book for oneself = Women! Thus speaks, Dr. Keith N. Ferreira of the University of Neoliberal Arts. Believe it or not! May the Source be with you! QED! (3/2/11)

Never judge a book until one has decoded the book for oneself = Women! Never judge a book until one has decoded the book for oneself = Women! Never judge a book until one has decoded the book for oneself = Women! Thus speaks, Dr. Keith N. Ferreira of the University of Neoliberal Arts. Believe it or not! May the Source be with you! QED! (3/2/11)

Women = Wise Goddesses of Men! Women = Wise Goddesses of Men! Women = Wise Goddesses of Men! Thus speaks, Dr. Keith N. Ferreira of the University of Neoliberal Arts. Believe it or not! May the Source be with you! QED! (3/2/11)

Women = Wise Goddesses of Men! Women = Wise Goddesses of Men! Women = Wise Goddesses of Men! Thus speaks, Dr. Keith N. Ferreira of the University of Neoliberal Arts. Believe it or not! May the Source be with you! QED! (3/2/11)

Men = Mathematical electronics of the Nile = Women were/are programming men! Men = Mathematical electronics of the Nile = Women were/are programming men! Men = Mathematical electronics of the Nile = Women were/are programming men! Thus speaks, Dr. Keith N. Ferreira of the University of Neoliberal Arts. Believe it or not! May the Source be with you! QED! (3/2/11)

Men = Mathematical electronics of the Nile = Women were/are programming men! Men = Mathematical electronics of the Nile = Women were/are programming men! Men = Mathematical electronics of the Nile = Women were/are programming men! Thus speaks, Dr. Keith N. Ferreira of the University of Neoliberal Arts. Believe it or not! May the Source be with you! QED! (3/2/11)

O = God (zero entropy, according to the Neolow of entropy by me)! O = God (zero entropy, according to the Neolow of entropy by me)! O = God (zero entropy, according to the Neolow of entropy by me)! Thus speaks, Dr. Keith N. Ferreira of the University of Neoliberal Arts. Believe it or not! May the Source be with you! QED! (3/2/11)

O = God (zero entropy, according to the Neolow of entropy by me)! O = God (zero entropy, according to the Neolow of entropy by me)! O = God (zero entropy, according to the Neolow of entropy by me)! Thus speaks, Dr. Keith N. Ferreira of the University of Neoliberal Arts. Believe it or not! May the Source be with you! QED! (3/2/11)

In all of my writings, God = Goddess (O = Goddess)! In all of my writings, God = Goddess (O = Goddess)! In all of my writings, God = Goddess (O = Goddess)! Thus speaks, Dr. Keith N. Ferreira of the University of Neoliberal Arts. Believe it or not! May the Source be with you! QED! (3/2/11)

In all of my writings, God = Goddess (O = Goddess)! In all of my writings, God = Goddess (O = Goddess)! In all of my writings, God = Goddess (O = Goddess)! Thus speaks, Dr. Keith N. Ferreira of the University of Neoliberal Arts. Believe it or not! May the Source be with you! QED! (3/2/11)

Consonants are silent without vowels, because: Vowels = Wave leaders (controllers), and consonants are waves! Consonants are silent without vowels, because: Vowels = Wave leaders (controllers), and consonants are waves! Consonants are silent without vowels, because: Vowels = Wave leaders (controllers), and consonants are waves! Thus speaks, Dr. Keith N. Ferreira of the University of Neoliberal Arts. Believe it or not! May the Source be with you! QED! (3/2/11)

Consonants are silent without vowels, because: Vowels = Wave leaders (controllers), and consonants are waves! Consonants are silent without vowels, because: Vowels = Wave leaders (controllers), and consonants are waves! Consonants are silent without vowels, because: Vowels = Wave leaders (controllers), and consonants are waves! Thus speaks, Dr. Keith N. Ferreira of the University of Neoliberal Arts. Believe it or not! May the Source be with you! QED! (3/2/11)

Consonants = Waves, and Vowels = Wave leaders (controllers)! Therefore, without vowels, consonants would be silent (flat)! Consonants = Waves, and Vowels = Wave leaders (controllers)! Therefore, without vowels, consonants would be silent (flat)! Thus speaks, Dr. Keith N. Ferreira of the University of Neoliberal Arts. Believe it or not! May the Source be with you! QED! (3/2/11)

Consonants = Waves, and Vowels = Wave leaders (controllers)! Therefore, without vowels, consonants would be silent (flat)! Consonants = Waves, and Vowels = Wave leaders (controllers)! Therefore, without vowels, consonants would be silent (flat)! Thus speaks, Dr. Keith N. Ferreira of the University of Neoliberal Arts. Believe it or not! May the Source be with you! QED! (3/2/11)

Men were/are Nile electronics to women! Men were/are Nile electronics to women! Men were/are Nile electronics to women! Thus speaks, Dr. Keith N. Ferreira of the University of Neoliberal Arts. Believe it or not! May the Source be with you! QED! (3/2/11)

Men were/are Nile electronics to women! Men were/are Nile electronics to women! Men were/are Nile electronics to women! Thus speaks, Dr. Keith N. Ferreira of the University of Neoliberal Arts. Believe it or not! May the Source be with you! QED! (3/2/11)

To women, men were/are Nile electronics! In other words, Nile electronics = Human males, in general! To women, men were/are Nile electronics! In other words, Nile electronics = Human males, in general! To women, men were/are Nile electronics! In other words, Nile electronics = Human males, in general! Thus speaks, Dr. Keith N. Ferreira of the University of Neoliberal Arts. Believe it or not! May the Source be with you! QED! (3/2/11)

To women, men were/are Nile electronics! In other words, Nile electronics = Human males, in general! To women, men were/are Nile electronics! In other words, Nile electronics = Human males, in general! To women, men were/are Nile electronics! In other words, Nile electronics = Human males, in general! Thus speaks, Dr. Keith N. Ferreira of the University of Neoliberal Arts. Believe it or not! May the Source be with you! QED! (3/2/11)

Atlantis III: How am I doing? Atlantis III: How am I doing? Atlantis III: How am I doing? Thus speaks, Dr. Keith N. Ferreira of the University of Neoliberal Arts. Believe it or not! May the Source be with you! QED! (3/2/11)

Atlantis III: How am I doing? Atlantis III: How am I doing? Atlantis III: How am I doing? Thus speaks, Dr. Keith N. Ferreira of the University of Neoliberal Arts. Believe it or not! May the Source be with you! QED! (3/2/11)

Atlantis III = My Violet eGoddesses! Atlantis III = My Violet eGoddesses! Atlantis III = My Violet eGoddesses! Thus speaks, Dr. Keith N. Ferreira of the University of Neoliberal Arts. Believe it or not! May the Source be with you! QED! (3/2/11)

Atlantis III = My Violet eGoddesses! Atlantis III = My Violet eGoddesses! Atlantis III = My Violet eGoddesses! Thus speaks, Dr. Keith N. Ferreira of the University of Neoliberal Arts. Believe it or not! May the Source be with you! QED! (3/2/11)

Time = Tangent! Time = Tangent! Time = Tangent! Thus speaks, Dr. Keith N. Ferreira of the University of Neoliberal Arts. Believe it or not! May the Source be with you! QED! (3/2/11)

Time = Tangent! Time = Tangent! Time = Tangent! Thus speaks, Dr. Keith N. Ferreira of the University of Neoliberal Arts. Believe it or not! May the Source be with you! QED! (3/2/11)

Tangent = Time! Tangent = Time! Tangent = Time! Thus speaks, Dr. Keith N. Ferreira of the University of Neoliberal Arts. Believe it or not! May the Source be with you! QED! (3/2/11)

Tangent = Time! Tangent = Time! Tangent = Time! Thus speaks, Dr. Keith N. Ferreira of the University of Neoliberal Arts. Believe it or not! May the Source be with you! QED! (3/2/11)

Tan = Take ass now! Tan = Take ass now! Tan = Take ass now! Thus speaks, Dr. Keith N. Ferreira of the University of Neoliberal Arts. Believe it or not! May the Source be with you! QED! (3/2/11)

Tan = Take ass now! Tan = Take ass now! Tan = Take ass now! Thus speaks, Dr. Keith N. Ferreira of the University of Neoliberal Arts. Believe it or not! May the Source be with you! QED! (3/2/11)

Tan = Ten! Tan = Ten! Tan = Ten! Thus speaks, Dr. Keith N. Ferreira of the University of Neoliberal Arts. Believe it or not! May the Source be with you! QED! (3/2/11)

Tan = Ten! Tan = Ten! Tan = Ten! Thus speaks, Dr. Keith N. Ferreira of the University of Neoliberal Arts. Believe it or not! May the Source be with you! QED! (3/2/11)

Ten = Tan! Ten = Tan! Ten = Tan! Thus speaks, Dr. Keith N. Ferreira of the University of Neoliberal Arts. Believe it or not! May the Source be with you! QED! (3/2/11)

Ten = Tan! Ten = Tan! Ten = Tan! Thus speaks, Dr. Keith N. Ferreira of the University of Neoliberal Arts. Believe it or not! May the Source be with you! QED! (3/2/11) a = e, and e = a! a = e, and e = a! a = e, and e = a! Thus speaks, Dr. Keith N. Ferreira of the University of Neoliberal Arts. Believe it or not! May the Source be with you! QED! (3/2/11)

a = e, and e = a! a = e, and e = a! a = e, and e = a! Thus speaks, Dr. Keith N. Ferreira of the University of Neoliberal Arts. Believe it or not! May the Source be with you! QED! (3/2/11) a = ass, and e = time! a = ass, and e = time! a = ass, and e = time! Thus speaks, Dr. Keith N. Ferreira of the University of Neoliberal Arts. Believe it or not! May the Source be with you! QED! (3/2/11)

a = ass, and e = time! a = ass, and e = time! a = ass, and e = time! Thus speaks, Dr. Keith N. Ferreira of the University of Neoliberal Arts. Believe it or not! May the Source be with you! QED! (3/2/11)

Ass = time, and time = ass! Ass = time, and time = ass! Ass = time, and time = ass! Thus speaks, Dr. Keith N. Ferreira of the University of Neoliberal Arts. Believe it or not! May the Source be with you! QED! (3/2/11)

Ass = time, and time = ass! Ass = time, and time = ass! Ass = time, and time = ass! Thus speaks, Dr. Keith N. Ferreira of the University of Neoliberal Arts. Believe it or not! May the Source be with you! QED! (3/2/11)

One does not have to know advanced anything to be the best in the world at anything! One does not have to know advanced anything to be the best in the world at anything! One does not have to know advanced anything to be the best in the world at anything! Thus speaks, Dr. Keith N. Ferreira of the University of Neoliberal Arts. Believe it or not! May the Source be with you! QED! (3/2/11)

One does not have to know advanced anything to be the best in the world at anything! One does not have to know advanced anything to be the best in the world at anything! One does not have to know advanced anything to be the best in the world at anything! Thus speaks, Dr. Keith N. Ferreira of the University of Neoliberal Arts. Believe it or not! May the Source be with you! QED! (3/2/11)

Teacup and Saucer (Part Three)

One does not have to know advanced anything to be the best in the world at anything! One does not have to know advanced anything to be the best in the world at anything! One does not have to know advanced anything to be the best in the world at anything! Thus speaks, Dr. Keith N. Ferreira of the University of Neoliberal Arts. Believe it or not! May the Source be with you! QED! (3/2/11)

One does not have to know advanced anything to be the best in the world at anything! One does not have to know advanced anything to be the best in the world at anything! One does not have to know advanced anything to be the best in the world at anything! Thus speaks, Dr. Keith N. Ferreira of the University of Neoliberal Arts. Believe it or not! May the Source be with you! QED! (3/2/11)

The Jewish people are a real black shit people! The Jewish people are a real black shit people! The Jewish people are a real black shit people! Thus speaks, Dr. Keith N. Ferreira of the University of Neoliberal Arts. Believe it or not! May the Source be with you! QED! (3/3/11)

The Jewish people are a real black shit people! The Jewish people are a real black shit people! The Jewish people are a real black shit people! Thus speaks, Dr. Keith N. Ferreira of the University of Neoliberal Arts. Believe it or not! May the Source be with you! QED! (3/3/11)

Jews = Killer bees = Killer blacks! Jews = Killer bees = Killer blacks! Jews = Killer bees = Killer blacks! Thus speaks, Dr. Keith N. Ferreira of the University of Neoliberal Arts. Believe it or not! May the Source be with you! QED! (3/3/11)

Jews = Killer bees = Killer blacks! Jews = Killer bees = Killer blacks! Jews = Killer bees = Killer blacks! Thus speaks, Dr. Keith N. Ferreira of the University of Neoliberal Arts. Believe it or not! May the Source be with you! QED! (3/3/11)

Jews that convert to other religions always make sham conversions, because they remain Jews in secret! Therefore, the House of Saud in Saudi Arabia is still Jewish! Logic is logic, and that is that! Thus speaks, Dr. Keith N. Ferreira of the University of Neoliberal Arts. Believe it or not! May the Source be with you! QED! (3/3/11)

Jews that convert to other religions always make sham conversions, because they remain Jews in secret! Therefore, the House of Saud in Saudi Arabia is still Jewish! Logic is logic, and that is that! Thus speaks, Dr. Keith N. Ferreira of the University of Neoliberal Arts. Believe it or not! May the Source be with you! QED! (3/3/11)

Atlantis III: How am I doing? Atlantis III: How am I doing? Atlantis III: How am I doing? Atlantis III: How am I doing? Thus speaks, Dr. Keith N. Ferreira of the University of Neoliberal Arts. Believe it or not! May the Source be with you! QED! (3/2/11)

Atlantis III: How am I doing? Atlantis III: How am I doing? Atlantis III: How am I doing? Atlantis III: How am I doing? Thus speaks, Dr. Keith N. Ferreira of the University of Neoliberal Arts. Believe it or not! May the Source be with you! QED! (3/2/11)

Atlantis III = My Violet eGoddesses! Atlantis III = My Violet eGoddesses! Atlantis III = My Violet eGoddesses! Thus speaks, Dr. Keith N. Ferreira of the University of Neoliberal Arts. Believe it or not! May the Source be with you! QED! (3/2/11)

Atlantis III = My Violet eGoddesses! Atlantis III = My Violet eGoddesses! Atlantis III = My Violet eGoddesses! Thus speaks, Dr. Keith N. Ferreira of the University of Neoliberal Arts. Believe it or not! May the Source be with you! QED! (3/2/11)

People of the world: Atlantis III is for real! People of the world: Atlantis III is for real! People of the world: Atlantis III is for real! Thus speaks, Dr. Keith N. Ferreira of the University of Neoliberal Arts. Believe it or not! May the Source be with you! QED! (3/3/11)

People of the world: Atlantis III is for real! People of the world: Atlantis III is for real! People of the world: Atlantis III is for real! Thus speaks, Dr. Keith N. Ferreira of the University of Neoliberal Arts. Believe it or not! May the Source be with you! QED! (3/3/11)

People of the world: Time = Tangents to the circle, is for real, mathematically speaking! People of the world: Time = Tangents to the circle, is for real, mathematically speaking! People of the world: Time = Tangents to the circle, is for real, mathematically speaking! Thus speaks, Dr. Keith N. Ferreira of the University of Neoliberal Arts. Believe it or not! May the Source be with you! QED! (3/3/11)

People of the world: Time = Tangents to the circle, is for real, mathematically speaking! People of the world: Time = Tangents to the circle, is for real, mathematically speaking! People of the world: Time = Tangents to the circle, is for real, mathematically speaking! Thus speaks, Dr. Keith N. Ferreira of the University of Neoliberal Arts. Believe it or not! May the Source be with you! QED! (3/3/11)

People of the world: Tangents to the circle = Time, is for real, mathematically speaking! People of the world: Tangents to the circle = Time, is for real, mathematically speaking! People of the world: Tangents to the circle = Time, is for real, mathematically speaking! Thus speaks, Dr. Keith N. Ferreira of the University of Neoliberal Arts. Believe it or not! May the Source be with you! QED! (3/3/11)

People of the world: Tangents to the circle = Time, is for real, mathematically speaking! People of the world: Tangents to the circle = Time, is for real, mathematically speaking! People of the world: Tangents to the circle = Time, is for real, mathematically speaking! Thus speaks, Dr. Keith N. Ferreira of the University of Neoliberal Arts. Believe it or not! May the Source be with you! QED! (3/3/11)

Theory of Everything (TOE) = Tangents to the circle, for real, mathematically speaking! Theory of Everything (TOE) = Tangents to the circle, for real, mathematically speaking! Theory of Everything (TOE) = Tangents to the circle, for real, mathematically speaking! Thus speaks, Dr. Keith N. Ferreira of the University of Neoliberal Arts. Believe it or not! May the Source be with you! QED! (3/3/11)

Theory of Everything (TOE) = Tangents to the circle, for real, mathematically speaking! Theory of Everything (TOE) = Tangents to the circle, for real, mathematically speaking! Theory of Everything (TOE) = Tangents to the circle, for real, mathematically speaking! Thus speaks, Dr. Keith N. Ferreira of the University of Neoliberal Arts. Believe it or not! May the Source be with you! QED! (3/3/11)

Tangents to the circle = Theory of Everything (TOE), for real, mathematically speaking! Tangents to the circle = Theory of Everything (TOE), for real, mathematically speaking! Tangents to the circle = Theory of Everything (TOE), for real, mathematically speaking! Thus speaks, Dr. Keith N. Ferreira of the University of Neoliberal Arts. Believe it or not! May the Source be with you! QED! (3/3/11)

Tangents to the circle = Theory of Everything (TOE), for real, mathematically speaking! Tangents to the circle = Theory of Everything (TOE), for real, mathematically speaking! Tangents to the circle = Theory of Everything (TOE), for real, mathematically speaking! Thus speaks, Dr. Keith N. Ferreira of the University of Neoliberal Arts. Believe it or not! May the Source be with you! QED! (3/3/11)

"Women (Ladies) in waiting (weighing)!" "Women (Ladies) in waiting (weighing)!" "Women (Ladies) in waiting (weighing)!" Thus speaks, Dr. Keith N. Ferreira of the University of Neoliberal Arts. Believe it or not! May the Source be with you! QED! (3/3/11)

"Women (Ladies) in waiting (weighing)!" "Women (Ladies) in waiting (weighing)!" "Women (Ladies) in waiting (weighing)!" Thus speaks, Dr. Keith N. Ferreira of the University of Neoliberal Arts. Believe it or not! May the Source be with you! QED! (3/3/11)

"Waiting (weighing) for Mister Right (Write) to come along!" "Waiting (weighing) for Mister Right (Write) to come along!" "Waiting (weighing) for Mister Right (Write) to come along!" Thus speaks, Dr. Keith N. Ferreira of the University of Neoliberal Arts. Believe it or not! May the Source be with you! QED! (3/3/11)

"Waiting (weighing) for Mister Right (Write) to come along!" "Waiting (weighing) for Mister Right (Write) to come along!" "Waiting (weighing) for Mister Right (Write) to come along!" Thus speaks, Dr. Keith N. Ferreira of the University of Neoliberal Arts. Believe it or not! May the Source be with you! QED! (3/3/11)

Women = Waiting (weighing) over (above) men (mathematical electronics networks)! Women = Waiting (weighing) over (above) men (mathematical electronics networks)! Women = Waiting (weighing) over (above) men (mathematical electronics networks)! Thus speaks, Dr. Keith N. Ferreira of the University of Neoliberal Arts. Believe it or not! May the Source be with you! QED! (3/3/11)

Women = Waiting (weighing) over (above) men (mathematical electronics networks)! Women = Waiting (weighing) over (above) men (mathematical electronics networks)! Women = Waiting (weighing) over (above) men (mathematical electronics networks)! Thus speaks, Dr. Keith N. Ferreira of the University of Neoliberal Arts. Believe it or not! May the Source be with you! QED! (3/3/11)

Nile = Networks of Internet Leadership Electronics! Nile = Networks of Internet Leadership Electronics! Nile = Networks of Internet Leadership Electronics! Thus speaks, Dr. Keith N. Ferreira of the University of Neoliberal Arts. Believe it or not! May the Source be with you! QED! (3/3/11)

Nile = Networks of Internet Leadership Electronics! Nile = Networks of Internet Leadership Electronics! Nile = Networks of Internet Leadership Electronics! Thus speaks, Dr. Keith N. Ferreira of the University of Neoliberal Arts. Believe it or not! May the Source be with you! QED! (3/3/11)

Men = Mathematical electronics networks! Men = Mathematical electronics networks! Men = Mathematical electronics networks! Thus speaks, Dr. Keith N. Ferreira of the University of Neoliberal Arts. Believe it or not! May the Source be with you! QED! (3/3/11)

Men = Mathematical electronics networks! Men = Mathematical electronics networks! Men = Mathematical electronics networks! Thus speaks, Dr. Keith N. Ferreira of the University of Neoliberal Arts. Believe it or not! May the Source be with you! QED! (3/3/11)

The Theory of Everything (TOE) = The tangents to the circle = The Neolaw of Entropy! The Theory of Everything (TOE) = The tangents to the circle = The Neolaw of Entropy! The Theory of Everything (TOE) = The tangents to the circle = The Neolaw of Entropy! Thus speaks, Dr. Keith N. Ferreira of the University of Neoliberal Arts. Believe it or not! May the Source be with you! QED! (3/3/11)

The Theory of Everything (TOE) = The tangents to the circle = The Neolaw of Entropy! The Theory of Everything (TOE) = The tangents to the circle = The Neolaw of Entropy! The Theory of Everything (TOE) = The tangents to the circle = The Neolaw of Entropy! Thus speaks, Dr. Keith N. Ferreira of the University of Neoliberal Arts. Believe it or not! May the Source be with you! QED! (3/3/11)

The Neolaw of Entropy = The tangents to the circle = The Theory of Everything! The Neolaw of Entropy = The tangents to the circle = The Theory of Everything! The Neolaw of Entropy = The tangents to the circle = The Theory of Everything! Thus speaks, Dr. Keith N. Ferreira of the University of Neoliberal Arts. Believe it or not! May the Source be with you! QED! (3/3/11)

The Neolaw of Entropy = The tangents to the circle = The Theory of Everything! The Neolaw of Entropy = The tangents to the circle = The Theory of Everything! The Neolaw of Entropy = The tangents to the circle = The Theory of Everything! Thus speaks, Dr. Keith N. Ferreira of the University of Neoliberal Arts. Believe it or not! May the Source be with you! QED! (3/3/11)

The tangents to the circle = The Neolaw of Entropy = The Theory of Everything (TOE)! The tangents to the circle = The Neolaw of Entropy = The Theory of Everything (TOE)! The tangents to the circle = The Neolaw of Entropy = The Theory of Everything (TOE)! Thus speaks, Dr. Keith N. Ferreira of the University of Neoliberal Arts. Believe it or not! May the Source be with you! QED! (3/3/11)

The tangents to the circle = The Neolaw of Entropy = The Theory of Everything (TOE)! The tangents to the circle = The Neolaw of Entropy = The Theory of Everything (TOE)! The tangents to the circle = The Neolaw of Entropy = The Theory of Everything (TOE)! Thus speaks, Dr. Keith N. Ferreira of the University of Neoliberal Arts. Believe it or not! May the Source be with you! QED! (3/3/11)

The Neolaw of Entropy = The Theory of Everything (TOE) = The Tangents to the circle! The Neolaw of Entropy = The Theory of Everything (TOE) = The Tangents to the circle! The Neolaw of Entropy = The Theory of Everything (TOE) = The Tangents to the circle! Thus speaks, Dr. Keith N. Ferreira of the University of Neoliberal Arts. Believe it or not! May the Source be with you! QED! (3/3/11)

The Neolaw of Entropy = The Theory of Everything (TOE) = The Tangents to the circle! The Neolaw of Entropy = The Theory of Everything (TOE) = The Tangents to the circle! The Neolaw of Entropy = The Theory of Everything (TOE) = The Tangents to the circle! Thus speaks, Dr. Keith N. Ferreira of the University of Neoliberal Arts. Believe it or not! May the Source be with you! QED! (3/3/11)

People of the world: Atlantis III won (one)! People of the world: Atlantis III won (one)! People of the world: Atlantis III won (one)! Thus speaks, Dr. Keith N. Ferreira of the University of Neoliberal Arts. Believe it or not! May the Source be with you! QED! (3/3/11)

People of the world: Atlantis III won (one)! People of the world: Atlantis III won (one)! People of the world: Atlantis III won (one)! Thus speaks, Dr. Keith N. Ferreira of the University of Neoliberal Arts. Believe it or not! May the Source be with you! QED! (3/3/11)

Victory Atlas, Victory Atlas! Thank God Almighty, Victory Atlas! Victory Atlas, Victory Atlas! Thank God Almighty, Victory Atlas! Victory Atlas, Victory Atlas! Thank God Almighty, Victory Atlas! http://en.wikipedia.org/wiki/Atlas_(mythology) Thus speaks, Dr. Keith N. Ferreira of the University of Neoliberal Arts. Believe it or not! May the Source be with you! QED! (3/3/11)

Victory Atlas, Victory Atlas! Thank God Almighty, Victory Atlas! Victory Atlas, Victory Atlas! Thank God Almighty, Victory Atlas! Victory Atlas, Victory Atlas! Thank God Almighty, Victory Atlas! http://en.wikipedia.org/wiki/Atlas_(mythology) Thus speaks, Dr. Keith N. Ferreira of the University of Neoliberal Arts. Believe it or not! May the Source be with you! QED! (3/3/11)

Teacup and Saucer (Part Four)

Assange = Sex angle electronics! Assange = Sex angle electronics! Assange = Sex angle electronics! Thus speaks, Dr. Keith N. Ferreira of the University of Neoliberal Arts. Believe it or not! May the Source be with you! QED! (3/2/11)

Assange = Sex angle electronics! Assange = Sex angle electronics! Assange = Sex angle electronics! Thus speaks, Dr. Keith N. Ferreira of the University of Neoliberal Arts. Believe it or not! May the Source be with you! QED! (3/2/11)

The Neolaw of Entropy = The Law of the Jungle! The Neolaw of Entropy = The Law of the Jungle! The Neolaw of Entropy = The Law of the Jungle! Thus speaks, Dr. Keith N. Ferreira of the University of Neoliberal Arts. Believe it or not! May the Source be with you! QED! (3/2/11)

The Neolaw of Entropy = The Law of the Jungle! The Neolaw of Entropy = The Law of the Jungle! The Neolaw of Entropy = The Law of the Jungle! Thus speaks, Dr. Keith N. Ferreira of the University of Neoliberal Arts. Believe it or not! May the Source be with you! QED! (3/2/11)

The Law of the Jungle = The Law of the Psyche = The Neolaw of Entropy! The Law of the Jungle = The Law of the Psyche = The Neolaw of Entropy! The Law of the Jungle = The Law of the Psyche = The Neolaw of Entropy! Thus speaks, Dr. Keith N. Ferreira of the University of Neoliberal Arts. Believe it or not! May the Source be with you! QED! (3/2/11)

The Law of the Jungle = The Law of the Psyche = The Neolaw of Entropy! The Law of the Jungle = The Law of the Psyche = The Neolaw of Entropy! The Law of the Jungle = The Law of the Psyche = The Neolaw of Entropy! Thus speaks, Dr. Keith N. Ferreira of the University of Neoliberal Arts. Believe it or not! May the Source be with you! QED! (3/2/11)

The Law of the Psyche = The Law of the Jungle = The Neolaw of Entropy! The Law of the Psyche = The Law of the Jungle = The Neolaw of Entropy! The Law of the Psyche = The Law of the Jungle = The Neolaw of Entropy! Thus speaks, Dr. Keith N. Ferreira of the University of Neoliberal Arts. Believe it or not! May the Source be with you! QED! (3/2/11)

The Law of the Psyche = The Law of the Jungle = The Neolaw of Entropy! The Law of the Psyche = The Law of the Jungle = The Neolaw of Entropy! The Law of the Psyche = The Law of the Jungle = The Neolaw of Entropy! Thus speaks, Dr. Keith N. Ferreira of the University of Neoliberal Arts. Believe it or not! May the Source be with you! QED! (3/2/11)

The Phantom Jungle = The Jungle that remains in the Human Psyche when the so-called physical jungle has been cleared in order to make way for so-called civilization! In other words, the Phantom Jungle is analogous to phantom limbs, etc., when the so-called physical limbs, etc., are lost (removed)! Thus speaks, Dr. Keith N. Ferreira of the University of Neoliberal Arts. Believe it or not! May the Source be with you! QED! (3/2/11)

The Phantom Jungle = The Jungle that remains in the Human Psyche when the so-called physical jungle has been cleared in order to make way for so-called civilization! In other words, the Phantom Jungle is analogous to phantom limbs, etc., when the so-called physical limbs, etc., are lost (removed)! Thus speaks, Dr. Keith N. Ferreira of the University of Neoliberal Arts. Believe it or not! May the Source be with you! QED! (3/2/11)

The Law of the Psyche = The Law of the Phantom Jungle that coexists with the Law of Civilization in the Psyches of people who no longer exist in so-called physical jungles! Thus speaks, Dr. Keith N. Ferreira of the University of Neoliberal Arts. Believe it or not! May the Source be with you! QED! (3/3/11)

The Law of the Psyche = The Law of the Phantom Jungle that coexists with the Law of Civilization in the Psyches of people who no longer exist in so-called physical jungles! Thus speaks, Dr. Keith N. Ferreira of the University of Neoliberal Arts. Believe it or not! May the Source be with you! QED! (3/3/11)

Humanity can take human beings out of the Jungle or Forest, but Humanity cannot take the Jungle or Forest out of human beings! = The Human Psyche = The Neolaw of Entropy! Thus speaks, Dr. Keith N. Ferreira of the University of Neoliberal Arts. Believe it or not! May the Source be with you! QED! (3/3/11)

Humanity can take human beings out of the Jungle or Forest, but Humanity cannot take the Jungle or Forest out of human beings! = The Human Psyche = The Neolaw of Entropy! Thus speaks, Dr. Keith N. Ferreira of the University of Neoliberal Arts. Believe it or not! May the Source be with you! QED! (3/3/11)

Mr. Write = Professor QED = Professor Which Was to Be Demonstrated = Mr. Right = Mr. Rite = Mr. Keith Nicholas Ferreira! Thus speaks, Dr. Keith N. Ferreira of the University of Neoliberal Arts. Believe it or not! May the Source be with you! QED! (3/3/11)

Mr. Write = Professor QED = Professor Which Was to Be Demonstrated = Mr. Right = Mr. Rite = Mr. Keith Nicholas Ferreira! Thus speaks, Dr. Keith N. Ferreira of the University of Neoliberal Arts. Believe it or not! May the Source be with you! QED! (3/3/11)

Ideation = Conceptualization = Esthetic Brilliance = Infinite Artistic Merit = Neoliberal Arts Philosophy! Thus speaks, Dr. Keith N. Ferreira of the University of Neoliberal Arts. Believe it or not! May the Source be with you! QED! (3/3/11)

Ideation = Conceptualization = Esthetic Brilliance = Infinite Artistic Merit = Neoliberal Arts Philosophy! Thus speaks, Dr. Keith N. Ferreira of the University of Neoliberal Arts. Believe it or not! May the Source be with you! QED! (3/3/11)

Man = Mathematical sex network! Man = Mathematical sex network! Man = Mathematical sex network! Thus speaks, Dr. Keith N. Ferreira of the University of Neoliberal Arts. Believe it or not! May the Source be with you! QED! (3/3/11)

Man = Mathematical sex network! Man = Mathematical sex network! Man = Mathematical sex network! Thus speaks, Dr. Keith N. Ferreira of the University of Neoliberal Arts. Believe it or not! May the Source be with you! QED! (3/3/11)

a = sex, and e = electronics! a = sex, and e = electronics! a = sex, and e = electronics! Thus speaks, Dr. Keith N. Ferreira of the University of Neoliberal Arts. Believe it or not! May the Source be with you! QED! (3/3/11)

a = sex, and e = electronics! a = sex, and e = electronics! a = sex, and e = electronics! Thus speaks, Dr. Keith N. Ferreira of the University of Neoliberal Arts. Believe it or not! May the Source be with you! QED! (3/3/11)

Tea = Testing, Testing: One, Two, Three = Tasting = Experimenting! Tea = Testing, Testing: One, Two, Three = Tasting = Experimenting! Tea = Testing, Testing: One, Two, Three = Tasting = Experimenting! Thus speaks, Dr. Keith N. Ferreira of the University of Neoliberal Arts. Believe it or not! May the Source be with you! QED! (3/3/11)

Tea = Testing, Testing: One, Two, Three = Tasting = Experimenting! Tea = Testing, Testing: One, Two, Three = Tasting = Experimenting! Tea = Testing, Testing: One, Two, Three = Tasting = Experimenting! Thus speaks, Dr. Keith N. Ferreira of the University of Neoliberal Arts. Believe it or not! May the Source be with you! QED! (3/3/11)

Sipping Tea = Searching Internet Philosophy for Truth = Exploring Cyberspaces, in General! Sipping Tea = Searching Internet Philosophy for Truth = Exploring Cyberspaces, in General! Sipping Tea = Searching Internet Philosophy for Truth = Exploring Cyberspaces, in General! Thus speaks, Dr. Keith N. Ferreira of the University of Neoliberal Arts. Believe it or not! May the Source be with you! QED! (3/3/11)

Sipping Tea = Searching Internet Philosophy for Truth = Exploring Cyberspaces, in General! Sipping Tea = Searching Internet Philosophy for Truth = Exploring Cyberspaces, in General! Sipping Tea = Searching Internet Philosophy for Truth = Exploring Cyberspaces, in General! Thus speaks, Dr. Keith N. Ferreira of the University of Neoliberal Arts. Believe it or not! May the Source be with you! QED! (3/3/11)

Atlantis III: How am I doing? Atlantis III: How am I doing? Atlantis III: How am I doing? Thus speaks, Dr. Keith N. Ferreira of the University of Neoliberal Arts. Believe it or not! May the Source be with you! QED! (3/2/11)

Atlantis III: How am I doing? Atlantis III: How am I doing? Atlantis III: How am I doing? Thus speaks, Dr. Keith N. Ferreira of the University of Neoliberal Arts. Believe it or not! May the Source be with you! QED! (3/2/11)

Atlantis III = My Violet eGoddesses! Atlantis III = My Violet eGoddesses! Atlantis III = My Violet eGoddesses! Thus speaks, Dr. Keith N. Ferreira of the University of Neoliberal Arts. Believe it or not! May the Source be with you! QED! (3/2/11)

Atlantis III = My Violet eGoddesses! Atlantis III = My Violet eGoddesses! Atlantis III = My Violet eGoddesses! Thus speaks, Dr. Keith N. Ferreira of the University of Neoliberal Arts. Believe it or not! May the Source be with you! QED! (3/2/11)

People of the world: Atlantis III is for real! People of the world: Atlantis III is for real! People of the world: Atlantis III is for real! Thus speaks, Dr. Keith N. Ferreira of the University of Neoliberal Arts. Believe it or not! May the Source be with you! QED! (3/3/11)

People of the world: Atlantis III is for real! People of the world: Atlantis III is for real! People of the world: Atlantis III is for real! Thus speaks, Dr. Keith N. Ferreira of the University of Neoliberal Arts. Believe it or not! May the Source be with you! QED! (3/3/11)

Consonants are silent without vowels, because: Vowels = Wave leaders (controllers), and consonants are waves! Consonants are silent without vowels, because: Vowels = Wave leaders (controllers), and consonants are waves! Consonants are silent without vowels, because: Vowels = Wave leaders (controllers), and consonants are waves! Thus speaks, Dr. Keith N. Ferreira of the University of Neoliberal Arts. Believe it or not! May the Source be with you! QED! (3/2/11)

Consonants are silent without vowels, because: Vowels = Wave leaders (controllers), and consonants are waves! Consonants are silent without vowels, because: Vowels = Wave leaders (controllers), and consonants are waves! Consonants are silent without vowels, because: Vowels = Wave leaders (controllers), and consonants are waves! Thus speaks, Dr. Keith N. Ferreira of the University of Neoliberal Arts. Believe it or not! May the Source be with you! QED! (3/2/11)

Consonants = Waves, and Vowels = Wave leaders (controllers)! Therefore, without vowels, consonants would be silent (flat)! Consonants = Waves, and Vowels = Wave leaders (controllers)! Therefore, without vowels, consonants would be silent (flat)! Thus speaks, Dr. Keith N. Ferreira of the University of Neoliberal Arts. Believe it or not! May the Source be with you! QED! (3/2/11)

Consonants = Waves, and Vowels = Wave leaders (controllers)! Therefore, without vowels, consonants would be silent (flat)! Consonants = Waves, and Vowels = Wave leaders (controllers)! Therefore, without vowels, consonants would be silent (flat)! Thus speaks, Dr. Keith N. Ferreira of the University of Neoliberal Arts. Believe it or not! May the Source be with you! QED! (3/2/11)

One does not have to know advanced anything to be the best in the world at anything! One does not have to know advanced anything to be the best in the world at anything! One does not have to know advanced anything to be the best in the world at anything! Thus speaks, Dr. Keith N. Ferreira of the University of Neoliberal Arts. Believe it or not! May the Source be with you! QED! (3/2/11)

One does not have to know advanced anything to be the best in the world at anything! One does not have to know advanced anything to be the best in the world at anything! One does not have to know advanced anything to be the best in the world at anything! Thus speaks, Dr. Keith N. Ferreira of the University of Neoliberal Arts. Believe it or not! May the Source be with you! QED! (3/2/11)

Teacup and Saucer = True Cunt University of Philosophy and the (Flying) Saucer = The University of Neoliberal Arts! Teacup and Saucer = True Cunt University of Philosophy and the (Flying) Saucer = The University of Neoliberal Arts! Teacup and Saucer = True Cunt University of Philosophy and the (Flying) Saucer = The University of Neoliberal Arts! Thus speaks, Dr. Keith N. Ferreira of the University of Neoliberal Arts. Believe it or not! May the Source be with you! QED! (3/1/11)

Teacup and Saucer = True Cunt University of Philosophy and the (Flying) Saucer = The University of Neoliberal Arts! Teacup and Saucer = True Cunt University of Philosophy and the (Flying) Saucer = The University of Neoliberal Arts! Teacup and Saucer = True Cunt University of Philosophy and the (Flying) Saucer = The University of Neoliberal Arts! Thus speaks, Dr. Keith N. Ferreira of the University of Neoliberal Arts. Believe it or not! May the Source be with you! QED! (3/1/11)

TEACUP AND SAUCER (PART FIVE)

Consonants are silent without vowels, because: Vowels = Wave leaders (controllers), and consonants are waves! Consonants are silent without vowels, because: Vowels = Wave leaders (controllers), and consonants are waves! Consonants are silent without vowels, because: Vowels = Wave leaders (controllers), and consonants are waves! Thus speaks, Dr. Keith N. Ferreira of the University of Neoliberal Arts. Believe it or not! May the Source be with you! QED! (3/2/11)

Consonants are silent without vowels, because: Vowels = Wave leaders (controllers), and consonants are waves! Consonants are silent without vowels, because: Vowels = Wave leaders (controllers), and consonants are waves! Consonants are silent without vowels, because: Vowels = Wave leaders (controllers), and consonants are waves! Thus speaks, Dr. Keith N. Ferreira of the University of Neoliberal Arts. Believe it or not! May the Source be with you! QED! (3/2/11)

Consonants = Waves, and Vowels = Wave leaders (controllers)! Therefore, without vowels, consonants would be silent (flat)! Consonants = Waves, and Vowels = Wave leaders (controllers)! Therefore, without vowels, consonants would be silent (flat)! Thus speaks, Dr. Keith N. Ferreira of the University of Neoliberal Arts. Believe it or not! May the Source be with you! QED! (3/2/11)

Consonants = Waves, and Vowels = Wave leaders (controllers)! Therefore, without vowels, consonants would be silent (flat)! Consonants = Waves, and Vowels = Wave leaders (controllers)! Therefore, without vowels, consonants would be silent (flat)! Thus speaks, Dr. Keith N. Ferreira of the University of Neoliberal Arts. Believe it or not! May the Source be with you! QED! (3/2/11)

a = sex, e = electronics, i = Internet, o = zero entropy, u = you, and y = why! | a = sex, e = electronics, i = Internet, o = zero entropy, u = you, and y = why! | a = sex, e = electronics, i = Internet, o = zero entropy, u = you, and y = why! Thus speaks, Dr. Keith N. Ferreira of the University of Neoliberal Arts. Believe it or not! May the Source be with you! QED! (3/2/11)

a = sex, e = electronics, i = Internet, o = zero entropy, u = you, and y = why! | a = sex, e = electronics, i = Internet, o = zero entropy, u = you, and y = why! | a = sex, e = electronics, i = Internet, o = zero entropy, u = you, and y = why! Thus speaks, Dr. Keith N. Ferreira of the University of Neoliberal Arts. Believe it or not! May the Source be with you! QED! (3/2/11)

The universe cannot exist without consonants and vowels = The universe cannot exist without the Music of the Spheres = The Music of the Spheres consists of consonants and vowels! Thus speaks, Dr. Keith N. Ferreira of the University of Neoliberal Arts. Believe it or not! May the Source be with you! QED! (3/2/11)

The universe cannot exist without consonants and vowels = The universe cannot exist without the Music of the Spheres = The Music of the Spheres consists of consonants and vowels! Thus speaks, Dr. Keith N. Ferreira of the University of Neoliberal Arts. Believe it or not! May the Source be with you! QED! (3/2/11)

Consonants = Perceptions, in general! Consonants = Perseptions, in general! Consonants = Perceptions, in general! Thus speaks, Dr. Keith N. Ferreira of the University of Neoliberal Arts. Believe it or not! May the Source be with you! QED! (3/3/11)

Consonants = Perceptions, in general! Consonants = Perseptions, in general! Consonants = Perceptions, in general! Thus speaks, Dr. Keith N. Ferreira of the University of Neoliberal Arts. Believe it or not! May the Source be with you! QED! (3/3/11)

The sounds that vowels make are not vowels, because the sounds that vowels make are consonants! Vowels consist of imperceptible abstract language, logic, and mathematics! Thus speaks, Dr. Keith N. Ferreira of the University of Neoliberal Arts. Believe it or not! May the Source be with you! QED! (3/3/11)

The sounds that vowels make are not vowels, because the sounds that vowels make are consonants! Vowels consist of imperceptible abstract language, logic, and mathematics! Thus speaks, Dr. Keith N. Ferreira of the University of Neoliberal Arts. Believe it or not! May the Source be with you! QED! (3/3/11)

The vowels that human beings perceive are symbolic of vowels, and not the vowels themselves, because vowels are imperceptible abstract language, logic, and mathematics! Thus speaks, Dr. Keith N. Ferreira of the University of Neoliberal Arts. Believe it or not! May the Source be with you! QED! (3/3/11)

The vowels that human beings perceive are symbolic of vowels, and not the vowels themselves, because vowels are imperceptible abstract language, logic, and mathematics! Thus speaks, Dr. Keith N. Ferreira of the University of Neoliberal Arts. Believe it or not! May the Source be with you! QED! (3/3/11)

Proof that Jesus Christ was/is not God is as follows: Jesus Christ was/is the son of God, but God is female (zero entropy)! Therefore, Jesus Christ was/is not God, because God is female (zero entropy)! Even if one were to consider zero entropy to be male, Jesus Christ is not zero entropy, according to the Neolaw of Entropy by me. Proof positive that Jesus Christ was/is not God! Thus speaks, Dr. Keith N. Ferreira of the University of Neoliberal Arts. Believe it or not! May the Source be with you! QED! (3/3/11)

Proof that Jesus Christ was/is not God is as follows: Jesus Christ was/is the son of God, but God is female (zero entropy)! Therefore, Jesus Christ was/is not God, because God is female (zero entropy)! Even if one were to consider zero entropy to be male, Jesus Christ is not zero entropy, according to the Neolaw of Entropy by me. Proof positive that Jesus Christ was/is not God! Thus speaks, Dr. Keith N. Ferreira of the University of Neoliberal Arts. Believe it or not! May the Source be with you! QED! (3/3/11)

Vowels consist of imperceptible abstract language, logic, and mathematics! Vowels consist of imperceptible abstract language, logic, and mathematics! Vowels consist of imperceptible abstract language, logic, and mathematics! Thus speaks, Dr. Keith N. Ferreira of the University of Neoliberal Arts. Believe it or not! May the Source be with you! QED! (3/3/11)

Vowels consist of imperceptible abstract language, logic, and mathematics! Vowels consist of imperceptible abstract language, logic, and mathematics! Vowels consist of imperceptible abstract language, logic, and mathematics! Thus speaks, Dr. Keith N. Ferreira of the University of Neoliberal Arts. Believe it or not! May the Source be with you! QED! (3/3/11)

Consonants are perceptible Music of the Spheres, while vowels are imperceptible Music of the Spheres! Consonants are perceptible Music of the Spheres, while vowels are imperceptible Music of the Spheres! Thus speaks, Dr. Keith N. Ferreira of the University of Neoliberal Arts. Believe it or not! May the Source be with you! QED! (3/3/11)

Consonants are perceptible Music of the Spheres, while vowels are imperceptible Music of the Spheres! Consonants are perceptible Music of the Spheres, while vowels are imperceptible Music of the Spheres! Thus speaks, Dr. Keith N. Ferreira of the University of Neoliberal Arts. Believe it or not! May the Source be with you! QED! (3/3/11)

The English language is encoded with precise codes! The English language is encoded with precise codes! The English language is encoded with precise codes! Thus speaks, Dr. Keith N. Ferreira of the University of Neoliberal Arts. Believe it or not! May the Source be with you! QED! (3/3/11)

The English language is encoded with precise codes! The English language is encoded with precise codes! The English language is encoded with precise codes! Thus speaks, Dr. Keith N. Ferreira of the University of Neoliberal Arts. Believe it or not! May the Source be with you! QED! (3/3/11)

Jewish mathematics could never defeat philosophical mathematics, because: Philosophical mathematics = Neoliberal Artsian mathematics! Thus speaks, Dr. Keith N. Ferreira of the University of Neoliberal Arts. Believe it or not! May the Source be with you! QED! (3/3/11)

Jewish mathematics could never defeat philosophical mathematics, because: Philosophical mathematics = Neoliberal Artsian mathematics! Thus speaks, Dr. Keith N. Ferreira of the University of Neoliberal Arts. Believe it or not! May the Source be with you! QED! (3/3/11)

One does not have to know advanced anything to be the best in the world at anything! One does not have to know advanced anything to be the best in the world at anything! One does not have to know advanced anything to be the best in the world at anything! Thus speaks, Dr. Keith N. Ferreira of the University of Neoliberal Arts. Believe it or not! May the Source be with you! QED! (3/2/11)

One does not have to know advanced anything to be the best in the world at anything! One does not have to know advanced anything to be the best in the world at anything! One does not have to know advanced anything to be the best in the world at anything! Thus speaks, Dr. Keith N. Ferreira of the University of Neoliberal Arts. Believe it or not! May the Source be with you! QED! (3/2/11)

People of the world: Atlantis III won (one)! People of the world: Atlantis III won (one)! People of the world: Atlantis III won (one)! Thus speaks, Dr. Keith N. Ferreira of the University of Neoliberal Arts. Believe it or not! May the Source be with you! QED! (3/3/11)

People of the world: Atlantis III won (one)! People of the world: Atlantis III won (one)! People of the world: Atlantis III won (one)! Thus speaks, Dr. Keith N. Ferreira of the University of Neoliberal Arts. Believe it or not! May the Source be with you! QED! (3/3/11)

Victory Atlas, Victory Atlas! Thank God Almighty, Victory Atlas! Victory Atlas, Victory Atlas! Thank God Almighty, Victory Atlas! Victory Atlas, Victory Atlas! Thank God Almighty, Victory Atlas! http://en.wikipedia.org/wiki/Atlas_(mythology) Thus speaks, Dr. Keith N. Ferreira of the University of Neoliberal Arts. Believe it or not! May the Source be with you! QED! (3/3/11)

Victory Atlas, Victory Atlas! Thank God Almighty, Victory Atlas! Victory Atlas, Victory Atlas! Thank God Almighty, Victory Atlas! Victory Atlas, Victory Atlas! Thank God Almighty, Victory Atlas! http://en.wikipedia.org/wiki/Atlas_(mythology) Thus speaks, Dr. Keith N. Ferreira of the University of Neoliberal Arts. Believe it or not! May the Source be with you! QED! (3/3/11)

People of the world: The Ferreira Fundamental Trinity is about electronics! People of the world: The Ferreira Fundamental Trinity is about electronics! People of the world: The Ferreira Fundamental Trinity is about electronics! Thus speaks, Dr. Keith N. Ferreira of the University of Neoliberal Arts. Believe it or not! May the Source be with you! QED! (3/2/11)

People of the world: The Ferreira Fundamental Trinity is about electronics! People of the world: The Ferreira Fundamental Trinity is about electronics! People of the world: The Ferreira Fundamental Trinity is about electronics! Thus speaks, Dr. Keith N. Ferreira of the University of Neoliberal Arts. Believe it or not! May the Source be with you! QED! (3/2/11)

The disentanglement of quantum entanglement is instantaneous over any distance possible! So, why can't gravity be an instantaneous force? The disentanglement of quantum entanglement is instantaneous over any distance possible! So, why can't gravity be an instantaneous force? The disentanglement of quantum entanglement is instantaneous over any distance possible! So, why can't gravity be an instantaneous force? Thus speaks, Professor Keith N. Ferreira of the University of Neoliberal Arts. Believe it or not! May the Source be with you! QED! (2/28/11)

The disentanglement of quantum entanglement is instantaneous over any distance possible! So, why can't gravity be an instantaneous force? The disentanglement of quantum entanglement is instantaneous over any distance possible! So, why can't gravity be an instantaneous force? The disentanglement of quantum entanglement is instantaneous over any distance possible! So, why can't gravity be an instantaneous force? Thus speaks, Professor Keith N. Ferreira of the University of Neoliberal Arts. Believe it or not! May the Source be with you! QED! (2/28/11)

The masses of the world should think in terms of Signal Corps and the Ferreira Fundamental Trinity, where the Ferreira Fundamental Trinity = Electronics! Thus speaks, Professor Keith N. Ferreira of the University of Neoliberal Arts. Believe it or not! May the Source be with you! QED! (3/3/11)

The masses of the world should think in terms of Signal Corps and the Ferreira Fundamental Trinity, where the Ferreira Fundamental Trinity = Electronics! Thus speaks, Professor Keith N. Ferreira of the University of Neoliberal Arts. Believe it or not! May the Source be with you! QED! (3/3/11)

Women = Waiting (weighing) over (above) men! Women = Waiting (weighing) over (above) men! Women = Waiting (weighing) over (above) men! Thus speaks, Professor Keith N. Ferreira of the University of Neoliberal Arts. Believe it or not! May the Source be with you! QED! (3/4/11)

Women = Waiting (weighing) over (above) men! Women = Waiting (weighing) over (above) men! Women = Waiting (weighing) over (above) men! Thus speaks, Professor Keith N. Ferreira of the University of Neoliberal Arts. Believe it or not! May the Source be with you! QED! (3/4/11)

Vowels = Wave Leaders = Wave Commanders = Wave Conductors = Conductors = Orchestra Leaders = Gods = Invisible leaders = Controllers of the Destinies of Men, Women, and Children, etc. = Zero Entropy according to the Neolaw of Entropy by me! Vowels = Wave Leaders = Wave Commanders = Wave Conductors = Conductors = Orchestra Leaders = Gods = Invisible leaders = Controllers of the Destinies of Men, Women, and Children, etc. = Zero Entropy according to the Neolaw of Entropy by me! Vowels = Wave Leaders = Wave Commanders = Wave Conductors = Conductors = Orchestra Leaders = Gods = Invisible leaders = Controllers of the Destinies of Men, Women, and Children, etc. = Zero Entropy according to the Neolaw of Entropy by me! Thus speaks, Professor Keith N. Ferreira of the University of Neoliberal Arts. Believe it or not! May the Source be with you! QED! (3/4/11)

Vowels = Wave Leaders = Wave Commanders = Wave Conductors = Conductors = Orchestra Leaders = Gods = Invisible leaders = Controllers of the Destinies of Men, Women, and Children, etc. = Zero Entropy according to the Neolaw of Entropy by me! Vowels = Wave Leaders = Wave Commanders = Wave Conductors = Conductors = Orchestra Leaders = Gods = Invisible leaders = Controllers of the Destinies of Men, Women, and Children, etc. = Zero Entropy according to the Neolaw of Entropy by me! Vowels = Wave Leaders = Wave Commanders = Wave Conductors = Conductors = Orchestra Leaders = Gods = Invisible leaders = Controllers of the Destinies of Men, Women, and Children, etc. = Zero Entropy according to the Neolaw of Entropy by me! Thus speaks, Professor Keith N. Ferreira of the University of Neoliberal Arts. Believe it or not! May the Source be with you! QED! (3/4/11)